My Emmaus Walk

✠

True Stories of Faith, Hope, and Inspiration

DEBRA TOMASELLI

authorHOUSE®

AuthorHouse™
1663 Liberty Drive
Bloomington, IN 47403
www.authorhouse.com
Phone: 1 (800) 839-8640

© 2018 Debra Tomaselli. All rights reserved.

No part of this book may be reproduced, stored in a retrieval system, or transmitted by any means without the written permission of the author.

Scripture taken from The Living Bible copyright © 1971 by Tyndale House Foundation. Used by permission of Tyndale House Publishers Inc., Carol Stream, Illinois 60188. All rights reserved. The Living Bible, TLB, and the The Living Bible logo are registered trademarks of Tyndale House Publishers.

Published by AuthorHouse 08/10/2018

ISBN: 978-1-5462-5426-3 (sc)
ISBN: 978-1-5462-5425-6 (e)

Library of Congress Control Number: 2018909189

Print information available on the last page.

Any people depicted in stock imagery provided by Getty Images are models, and such images are being used for illustrative purposes only.
Certain stock imagery © Getty Images.

This book is printed on acid-free paper.

Because of the dynamic nature of the Internet, any web addresses or links contained in this book may have changed since publication and may no longer be valid. The views expressed in this work are solely those of the author and do not necessarily reflect the views of the publisher, and the publisher hereby disclaims any responsibility for them.

CONTENTS

Introduction vii

1. I Can't Wait to Tell You 1
2. What's in a meal? 4
3. You're Not Alone...We're Never Alone 7
4. The Job Search 10
5. What is the greatest goal of parenting? 13
6. Evangelization 101 16
7. 36 Years and Counting...a Tribute to My Husband 19
8. The Lessons of Summer 22
9. Blessed Mother, are you there? 24
10. Be strong! Be courageous! 27
11. The Black Leotard 30
12. The Guest Speaker 33
13. Who Knew We Couldn't Wait to Visit Dad? 36
14. The Prayer of a Summer Vacation 38
15. Balance Beam Wonders 41
16. Be careful what you pray for. 44

17. A Lesson in Divine Economy is Good for the Soul 47
18. Leaping Lizards…How'd we get here?? 50
19. Hovering Wings 53
20. Try it…Will you let God bless you? 56
21. Why Doesn't Somebody Help? 59
22. Angels in Disguise 62
23. Want to make a little change for the New Year? 65
24. What Was I Thinking? 68
25. When something seems like forever…maybe it's not! 71
26. Dear God, what's in a name? 74
27. What I learned from a kid's science lesson 77
28. What's the most embarrassing thing ever happened to you? 80
29. God Loves You and So Do I 83
30. God's power--perfected in our weaknesses? 86
31. Let the Windfall Where It May 89
32. Oh, Say, Can You See the Emerging Beauty? 92
33. He's Still the Reason for the Season 95
34. Welcome to the New Year…Are you singing a new song? 98
35. Homeward Bound 101
36. The Power of a Praying Mother 104

INTRODUCTION

Years ago, I struggled with a lengthy illness. Cancer was the suspect.

While hospitalized, I randomly opened my bible and read: "What I tell you now in the gloom, shout abroad when daybreak comes." (Matthew 10:27)

The verse felt prophetic.

I was too weak to even sit up straight, but I felt strengthened.

"I'm going to be alright," I thought. *"This is not going to be the cancer. It doesn't say 'if' daybreak comes, it says 'when' daybreak comes..."*

Crazy. I'd been journaling for years. Recently, though, I felt compelled to get published.

"...and my shouting abroad?" I closed my eyes. *"That's my writing."*

Thankfully, the mysterious illness wasn't cancer. As good health returned, I chose not to resume my former responsibilities. Instead, I focused on writing.

My first published piece appeared in Together in Christ. It was a reflection about how difficult it was to wait for good health to return on God's timetable, not my own.

The floodgates opened. The Upper Room published my work. The Word Among Us and On Mission magazine followed. I began writing nonstop about God's presence in everyday life...describing those 'aha' moments that are too miraculous to be anything else.

One day I met with a local editor. While pitching my idea for a monthly column, the proposed title suddenly surfaced and beginning May, 2003, my Emmaus Walk column was born.

I chose 'Emmaus Walk' after the biblical story in which, shortly after Christ's crucifixion, two saddened and confused disciples were walking from Jerusalem to Emmaus. (Luke 24:13-35) A stranger joins them, discussing scripture in light of the recent events. He's compelling, so they ask the stranger to stay and eat. In the breaking of the bread, they recognize him: He's the resurrected Christ.

This book is about that. It's about you. It's about us. It's about our road to Emmaus. We're walking along. We're at work, raising our kids, getting a haircut...and who shows up? God himself.

This book is a collection of my columns. The stories run the gamut of my life, including reflections from childhood, stories of motherhood, and even a few observations from the pleasures of grandparenting.

The central thread, however, is God's presence in the ordinary details of our days...and the freedom faith provides. These true stories illuminate God's consistent care...how he infinitely loves each one of us...and that getting to know his voice in our lives is the most valuable treasure we can discover...

I hope these stories inspire you. I hope they increase your faith. I hope they give you hope.

Go ahead. Turn the page. Let's share this journey together.

I Can't Wait to Tell You

"You should write a book," she said. "Have you ever thought about that?"

I smiled quietly and nodded. "Yes," I said. "I've heard that before."

"No, really," she added. "You need to write a book. Don't wait. Write it now."

Goosebumps covered me. Was she right?

My love affair with writing started early. I was elated when my fifth-grade teacher held a conference with my mom and me. "She's a gifted writer," Mrs. Koch said. "Don't let this talent be wasted."

English essays were simple. Writing was fun. I kept diaries and journals, scribbling daily notes. They communicated the ebb and flow of life.

As a young adult, I was offered an insurance job. Since I wanted to become a writer, I raced to the library and studied several authors' biographies. Many began publishing later in life, so I accepted the insurance position, realizing that if I didn't write now, it didn't mean I never would.

Little did I know, but God was at work.

Life got busy with marriage and the birth of our three daughters. Then, in a few short years, I lost my parents to cancer and my beloved younger brother to an early death.

Grief swallowed me. I struggled in the aftermath, thinking I'd never be happy again.

Despite my anger at God, I kept going to church. Maybe it was habit. Maybe I had nothing better to do. However, I began to notice that this was the only place I felt at peace.

Faith bloomed. It was the only answer to my grief. I joined bible studies, frequented the sacraments and prayed daily. As I rose from the ashes, all I could see was God's glorious presence.

A few years later, when I was diagnosed with cancer, I prayed with confidence: "Thy will, not mine, be done." Strangely, the scary diagnosis was a blessing. It shifted my perspective, propelling me to seek God's presence in my daily life.

With that, my childhood passion was revitalized. I began writing.

My first published piece, a reflection about how difficult it was to wait for good health to return on God's timetable rather than my own, appeared in "Together in Christ."

The stories flowed. I recorded my fears and God's responses. Others could relate…and my Emmaus Walk column was born.

It wasn't until I attended a Writers Conference in Arizona, however, that I realized the purpose of my writing. During introductions, we were asked why we write. There were mixed responses, but I didn't think twice. My answer came quickly and without hesitation:

"To show people how much God loves them."

That's why I write. God loves you so very much. There's a story to be told. I can't wait to tell you.

What's in a meal?

Sometimes ordinary actions make profound statements.

Like the day I arrived home from school and found my mother at work in the kitchen, wearing an apron. Puzzled, I cocked my head. Aprons were typically reserved for holidays.

She hugged me.

"Hurry and do your homework," Mom said, wiping her hands on a checkered dishtowel. "Father Ryan is coming over tonight."

My heart jumped. Really? Our pastor was coming to visit us?

We'd just moved to Las Cruces, New Mexico, and joined Holy Cross parish, where my brothers and I attended school. My parents had invited Father Ryan to dinner.

I threw my books on the sofa and followed my nose into the kitchen. There, Mom, glancing at a cookbook, was preparing chicken.

"What's that," I asked.

"Apricot chicken," she said. She squared her shoulders. "It's a new recipe I found."

I frowned.

"You'll like it," she promised. "Don't you and your brothers eat the last piece. Leave some in case our guest wants a second helping."

I scanned the countertop. There were fresh rolls waiting to bake, real butter, and makings for a chocolate cream pie, my personal favorite.

Dad came home from work early. It's the only time I remember him helping set the table, as he and Mom arranged linens, fine silver and china plates.

The doorbell rang and Father Ryan arrived, wearing a broad brimmed cowboy hat, which he removed upon entering our home. My brothers and I stared at him like he was a movie star while he and my parents exchanged greetings.

Later, we took our places at the dining room table. My brothers and I remembered our manners. My parents and Father Ryan found much in common, and their conversation was sprinkled with laughter.

When Father Ryan left, he donned his hat. Smiling, he welcomed us to the parish and thanked my parents for the enjoyable evening. It felt like a holiday. I got to stay up late on a school night.

Now, decades later, that evening remains a vivid memory.

While it wasn't distributed in a single meal, that evening represented the faith my parents treasured and offered to me. I'm thankful for that. We attended Mass every Sunday and holyday, stood in confessional lines on Saturdays, celebrated sacraments, and prayed as a family. My parents showed us how to listen, help, forgive and sacrifice for each other. They taught us to help others by donating clothes we'd outgrown and stocking food pantries for the needy.

Looking back, I learned never to underestimate the value of your actions of faith. Simple everyday deeds, like that of a meal, can be a powerful witness to a child, a co-worker, a neighbor or a priest.

Wherever you find yourself, whatever you are doing, you can reach people with the Gospel message. There's nothing more important than that.

And he told them, "You are to go into all the world and preach the Good News to everyone, everywhere." Mark 16:15

You're Not Alone...We're Never Alone

I'll never forget the moment.

I was a teenager, riding home from an outing to White Sands National Monument sponsored by our church's youth group. Since my family had just moved to New Mexico, my parents, hoping I'd meet other kids, signed me up for the trip.

We met at the church, boarded a school bus, and chose seats. Being the new kid, I ended up alone, with an entire row to myself.

The bus chugged its way across the highway to our destination. When we arrived, I was amazed at the desolation of the desert and the towering sand dunes. At White Sands, the dunes are sparkling white, and they made a striking contrast against a stark blue sky.

The bus parked and the leaders directed us, handed out kickballs and sleds, and set up food tables.

Some kids gathered and talked. Some played kickball. Others, like me, raced to the top of the dunes, hopped on the makeshift cardboard sleds and raced down.

I met Madelyn, a girl who was also going into seventh grade. Both of us had brothers, detested Math, and liked sports.

I spoke with Danny, a talented athlete who made us laugh, and Mary, who was popular.

However, meeting the new kids heightened my loneliness.

Back then, there was no Facebook. No internet. No texting. I missed my old friends.

I climbed a dune and surveyed the barren desert. It stretched as far as the eye could see. There was no sign of life. No movement. No sound. It was silence like I'd never heard before.

There was desolate beauty in this place.

At dinnertime, the leaders placed me in Mary's group.

When we boarded the bus for home, I returned to my solitary row.

Our leaders took roll call. They led us in prayer, thanking God for the beauty of the day.

Then the engine rumbled to life, and the big yellow bus rambled onto the highway. A full moon lit the way home.

I cranked my window down, and cool air billowed through.

On the way, I pondered my circumstances, which felt as bleak as the desert we'd just visited. As I struggled with loneliness, something suddenly changed.

My Emmaus Walk

Abruptly, sitting there in that bus, none of that mattered.

Suddenly, I felt filled with the greatest love imaginable.

It wasn't like parental love, nor was it like a crush for a cute boy.

It was greater than all of that.

I felt complete. I felt secure. I felt bubble-wrapped in love.

I felt happy, but I didn't know why. It took nearly a lifetime for me to realize that on that day, in the midst of desolation…God showed up.

And throughout my life, time and again, i good times and difficulties, and even now, as I battle cancer, he's revealed himself to me, filling me with courage, strength, love and unimaginable peace.

Oh, how he longs for us to recognize his omnipresent image.

Finally, I do.

The Job Search

"Get out of the car and don't return until you've knocked on every door in this building," my mother instructed me. She parked beside a three-story office complex.

"This is dumb," I said, yanking the car door open. "They probably don't need to hire anyone!"

My complaint landed on deaf ears.

"I'll be waiting for you," she said firmly. "Be sure to knock on every single door."

My recent graduation pushed me toward employment. Although I wanted office work, I dreaded the job search.

This was before internet days. You found jobs through classifieds, knocking on doors, completing applications and face-to-face interviews.

I cringed at the thought, bolstered by endless excuses: There weren't any good jobs in the classifieds. I didn't own a car yet. I didn't have work experience. I didn't know if I'd like the co-workers....

Finally, Mom, convinced I'd wrinkle and turn grey before finding employment, took charge. She made a plan: I'd dress for an interview and she'd take me on a job search. She claimed there were jobs available besides those in the classifieds. She knew where the nearby offices were. She would drive me there. When they saw my motivation, they'd waive the prior experience requirement. She knew they'd be reputable businesses and she knew the employees would be nice.

There was no escaping her plan.

I entered the building, breathed deeply, and opened the first door.

"I'm here to apply for a job," I said.

"We don't have any openings," the receptionist said.

After this happened several times, I relaxed. I was right after all.

Somewhat smug, I advanced to the second floor. The elevator opened to the lobby of a large office.

"I'd like to apply for a job," I said.

The receptionist handed me an application, which I completed. She disappeared, returning with a question.

"Do you have time to take a test?"

"Sure," I said.

I breezed through the quiz. Moments later she announced a manager would like to interview me. I agreed, making myself comfortable.

"By the way," I said. "What kind of an office is this?"

"Insurance," she replied.

Aetna Insurance offered me a job that day and a career that lasted a lifetime.

I bought my first car while working for Aetna, moved to Florida with Kemper Insurance, then joined an insurance agency. When I married and had children, I left fulltime work to create an independent, flexible schedule. I used my insurance skills to train employees, create continuing education programs and alleviate work overflows.

Years later, when I returned to fulltime insurance, a wonderful opportunity arose. It's close to home. It's a caring firm. I like my coworkers.

A lifetime ago, as I stepped out of my mom's car, who could have guessed this opportunity awaited me? Looking back, I realize that moment was graced with divine direction.

As strains of Pomp and Circumstance fade in the distance, I wish the same for today's graduates. I pray they have eyes to view the opportunities from above, and the wisdom to see, as the years roll by, the Hand that is holding theirs.

What is the greatest goal of parenting?

"I want a divorce."

Hearing my mom say that to my dad is one of my worst childhood memories. I lay in bed, surrounded by darkness, hoping I'd heard wrong.

Late night arguments had become the norm. Often, hungry for dinner, my brother and I would hover in the backyard, hearing their muffled quarrels from inside the house until long past dusk.

My parents, native New Yorkers, had recently moved to New Mexico after Dad accepted a promotion to relocate and become an engineer on the prestigious Apollo program.

Initially, it was enchanting. Mom delved into Southwestern history, planning family outings to ancient Mexican cathedrals, Carlsbad Caverns and White Sands.

But things changed.

Dad, who enjoyed a stellar promotion, worked long hours. He joined a carpool that frequented the local tavern after work, something he'd never done before. He enjoyed the popularity of his position.

While Dad was having fun, my brothers and I made new friends at Holy Cross Catholic School.

Mom, however, felt disconnected. Back then, long distance calls were rare. There was no Facetime, texting or Facebook. Additionally, the tight-knit community resisted the influx of New Yorkers. Although Mom hosted dinners for Dad's coworkers' families, it didn't replace the warmth of our beloved grandparents.

It had to be hard.

But divorce? I lay in the dark, trembling. My stomach churned. I cried, wishing I hadn't heard those cold words.

The next morning, getting ready for school, I held my breath, waiting for the big announcement. But it never came.

Instead, Dad dropped the carpool, and shortened his workday. Mom volunteered at school and made new friends. We attended every church event our parish held.

My parents chose to live their vows.

Love is patient – even when things aren't going your way. Love is kind – even when you are irritated. Love is not self-seeking-no matter how justified you feel.

Peace reigned, not just for them, but for us kids.

That Christmas, Dad gave Mom a mink stole. She pranced in delight. Dad took her hand and they embraced, dipped and kissed like newlyweds on the dance floor. I felt so happy.

Mom and Dad enjoyed a beautiful life together. Although there were more out-of-state moves, more sacrifices and more adjustments, they came easier, wrapped in faith and tempered with an air of selflessness.

Recently, while listening to a Laudate podcast, I thought of them. It referenced Matthew 19:14, "Let the little children come to me. Do not hinder them."

It's the parents' responsibility to bring their children to Jesus, the commentator said, and failure to live an authentic Christian life would hinder them. Actions speak louder than words. The greatest goal, he added, is for your child to reach heaven and hear them say, "Thank you for helping me get here."

I recalled the crossroad my parents faced long ago and the resulting impact of their actions.

Throughout my life, my faith has carried me. It shines through the good times and the bad, the joys and the sorrows, in sickness and in health. It provides a bit of heaven right here on earth.

Thanks, Mom and Dad, for helping me get here.

Evangelization 101

It was such a simple gesture, really, but one with infinite implications.

"Stop running," I shouted at my daughter as she raced through the living room.

"What can we do," she asked, wrestling her younger sister Jenna to the floor. "Can we watch TV?"

"Sure, you can watch cartoons," I mumbled. Lynn, 7, flipped on the television, while Jenna, 3, jumped into the bean bag chair. My husband was travelling on business, the baby was napping, and I was relieved the TV would entertain the girls. I flopped onto the sofa, oblivious to the dirty dishes in the sink, smelly clothes in the hamper and stack of mail accumulating on the table.

Suddenly there was a knock at my door. I jumped up, wondering who it could be. I ran my fingers through my tangled hair, smoothed my wrinkled shorts and searched for my shoes, surprised that anyone would have stopped by, unannounced, on a Sunday morning. Certainly, it was nobody important. I considered ignoring the caller, but the kids raced for the door and swung it open before I could stop them.

My Emmaus Walk

"Hi Deb," Wendy chirped. She was standing on my doorstep, surrounded by sunshine and blue skies. The rush of a cool breeze ushered its way in as I stood there, staring at her.

I barely knew Wendy. At least, she'd never been to my home before. We met recently while volunteering in our kids' computer classes at our parish school.

Like me, she had three children, the oldest of whom attended school together. Like me, her husband traveled on business. Like me, she enjoyed chatting after Mass while the kids played tag in the grotto.

But she was just an acquaintance. I didn't really know Wendy well, and I was surprised to see her on my doorstep. I just stood there, speechless.

"I noticed you weren't at church today," she said, "so I brought you this." Wendy handed me the weekly bulletin from our parish.

With that, I invited her in. She didn't stay long and I don't even recall what the conversation was about. Perhaps I admitted that I was struggling with grief from the recent death of my younger brother. Maybe I never mentioned it. I don't remember.

What I do recall is this: Someone cared enough to show up on my doorstep. Someone, in the name of the Lord, extended a hand to me when I needed it most. Someone stepped out of their comfort zone to bring the Church to me.

I was angry at God when Jim died. I often skipped church. I doubted my faith. It was a long and perilous journey back. Many glorious moments lit the way, but even now, some twenty years later, Wendy's simple act of evangelization shines brightly. Her humble gesture provided direction, hope and inspiration during a critical crossroad in my life. I doubt Wendy had a clue.

This Sunday, they'll be distributing bulletins after church. Maybe it's time for me to make a special delivery…one with everlasting benefits.

36 Years and Counting...a Tribute to My Husband

When I think of you, Joe, I think of you as my friend...my love...the father of our awesome children.

You've taught me so much about the meaning of family. From the minute I first met you, I knew you were special. I knew you were the one.

Family has always been #1 to you. I remember when we were dating, and we'd always travel to your home in New Hampshire for Christmas. Right off the bat, I remember going shopping with you for presents for your nieces and nephews. Yes, you were in a store. Probably in a mall, can't remember that part. You were so generous. That told me a lot about you right then and there.

It's no mistake you are the man God chose for me to marry. I love you, my dear. I'm thankful for all the times you've put me on the right track.

I remember going to you when I'd made a poor parenting decision that left a child frustrated. "Help me out," I'd say. You'd step in and save the day.

I also remember once, when the kids were young and I was trying to control too tightly, you just looked at me and said, "Why does everything have to be an argument? Let her do it." It was something silly, and, as they grew, you showed me how to let go of the control stick while still hanging onto the love threads.

Sometimes, though, I had to stick to my guns. Knowing this was my job, you always backed me up. We love you for that. I mean, after all, look at the end products...three beautiful daughters, a couple of loving sons-in-laws, and some incredible grandchildren. Pretty amazing, right?

You are freakishly smart. You know everything. You understood all that financial planning talk about compounding interest. You know who won the World Series in 1972 and 1985 and 2011. You remember the details surrounding political figures whose name I've never heard of.

You successfully set some amazing goals. How'd you do that? Catholic school educations for all kids? Helping them graduate from college debt-free? Here we are, in early retirement, shall I say, debt-free and still sipping chocolate sodas from Steak N Shake?

You're so quiet about all that...so humble. On the outside, you like to defer attention and make jokes. Inside, you are rock-solid. You are loyal. You are faith-filled. You know right from wrong. You are determined, decisive and confident. You are loving. You are unswerving. I love you for it.

When things get scary and I want to run, you step in. You are my strength when I am weak.

I love you so much. I'm so happy to be sharing life with you! Whatever may happen, I know that, together, with God at the helm, we can overcome it.

I, Debra, take you, Joe, to be my lawfully wedded husband, to have and to hold from this day forward, for better or for worse, for richer, for poorer, in sickness and in health, to love and to cherish, from this day forward, until death do us part.

The Lessons of Summer

"Forget it," my daughter said, flopping onto the sofa. "Nobody wants my help." Her eyes swelled with tears.

For months, Sara, 13, anticipated babysitting a 'baby' during her summer break. The dream was persistent and unrelenting.

Sara didn't care about earning money, she simply loved babies. But she needed to find one to watch. She distributed flyers, but to no avail. Our church nursery didn't need help, most of my contacts had outgrown infant stages, and day cares weren't interested in volunteers younger than eighteen years old.

I helped her search for a volunteer position, but when I found myself calling homeless shelters to see if they needed child-care assistance, I knew I'd lost my perspective.

After all, as determined as Sara was about caring for an infant, I didn't really want to leave our daughter just anywhere. She, too, needed a safe and enriching environment in which to spend her time.

Discouraged, I wanted to give up, too.

But wanting what was best for my child, and realizing she'd be miserable if her dream didn't materialize, I couldn't surrender. I had to persist.

"Let's pray," I suggested. I reached out and held her hand.

"Dear Lord," I began. "You know the desires of Sara's heart. You know somebody out there would love to have help with a baby and you know how Sara would like to help somebody. If it be your will, please connect us. If not, please help us find something else meaningful for her to do this summer. Amen."

I leaned back in my chair. She smiled. "It's in God's hands now," I said.

A moment later, I glanced down at the yellow pages, flopped open on my lap. My gaze landed on a small boxed ad: Redeemer Lutheran Day Care. I figured I could make one last call.

That call led to a church nursery. The director met with us, and, even though they didn't typically use teen volunteers, she gave Sara a chance to assist in the infant room. The setting ended up being perfect for her and for them. The director admitted that she wished they could pay Sara, as she was so helpful. Sara said she'd rather not get money, as the ability to work with the infants was reward in itself.

Sara grew in confidence and independence that summer. She learned a lot about working with other adults, and about caring for babies. But the lesson extended far beyond child care. What she discovered through that experience reached into the heavenly realms.

Blessed Mother, are you there?

As soon as I let Jenna, 9, race across the field to join Aunt Gina and Cousin Jenny, Sara, 5, exploded.

"Why can't I go with them," she demanded. But they'd already disappeared.

We'd traveled long to reach our destination, a remote hillside where a visionary reportedly was receiving messages from the Blessed Mother.

We'd been there before, Gina and me. Sitting on a hillside praying the rosary with thousands of pilgrims proved a powerful experience, one we wanted to share with our kids.

So we knew to arrive the night before, spread a blanket, and return early the next morning.

Gina and I went in opposite directions…her to the bookstore and me to spread our blanket for the next day. We'd meet at the car.

It was a pleasant afternoon with a gentle breeze but walking across the field with Sara screaming alongside me couldn't have been more horrid. She balked, pulled, pushed, and cried.

My Emmaus Walk

She was hungry. She was tired. She'd rather be with her sister and her cousin. I set my face like flint to get the job done.

When we finally reached our destination, I tossed the rumpled blanket onto the grass. As I did, I overheard the chatter of a small group nearby.

"Do you see it?" one woman shouted.

"Yes, I do!" a man exclaimed.

"Look at that!" another cried.

A hush fell over the group, but I didn't look up. I'd been here before when others experienced the 'miracle of the sun', but I could never see it. Instead, I feverishly worked to get the blanket arranged.

Suddenly I felt Sara silently tugging at my shorts.

I looked at her.

Her eyes were transfixed on the sun. Her shoulders were relaxed, the tears dried, her little fists unclenched. She seemed to be in another world.

"Do you see it?" I asked.

Speechless, she nodded. I followed her gaze upward, but the glare of the sun turned me away.

I looked back at Sara, still staring aloft.

"What do you see?" I asked.

Without blinking, she responded. "It's spinning," then added, "I see colors around the sun."

A hush settled over us. By the time I finished arranging the blanket, Sara no longer felt drawn to stare at the sun. It was like she re-entered this world, a changed child.

We held hands, skipped and laughed as we headed to the car. When we saw Aunt Gina and the girls, we couldn't wait to tell them what happened.

The rest of the evening was uneventful. We ate McDonalds, where the kids played, munched hamburgers and sipped milkshakes.

Some question whether the visionary was fabricating the messages or not. It never mattered to me. The prayerful experiences affected my life. But, honestly, I believe a five-year-old couldn't have manufactured the experience Sara had on that hillside that day.

Blessed Mother, pray for us.

Editor's note: The miracle of the sun reportedly occurred at Fatima, Portugal on October 13, 1917 when the Blessed Mother, appearing to three children, promised to send a sign "so all would believe." That day, thousands witnessed an opaque sun, surrounded by colors, spinning in the sky.

P.S. Catholics don't worship the Blessed Mother. She's just an awesome role model.

Be strong! Be courageous!

"Bye, Mom, see you in a few…" Sara hopped out of my car, slinging her backpack over one shoulder. "Remember not to feel bad if the kids don't pay attention," she said. "They're kind of like that to everyone."

She raced across the courtyard, disappearing into her seventh-grade classroom at St. Mary Magdalen Catholic School. Soon the door would reopen, and the teacher would signal for me to join them.

Suddenly, fear arose. *Why had I agreed to address the class about my recent illness? What if the kids ridiculed me…or, worse yet, what if they alienated Sara? What if my message got distorted, focusing attention on my situation instead of God?* I wanted to bolt, but it was too late; the commitment was made. Nervously I flipped open my Bible.

"Be strong! Be courageous!" Moses exhorted Joshua in Deuteronomy 31:7, "For you shall lead these people into the land promised by the Lord to their ancestors; see to it that they conquer it."

How perfect was that? I needed encouragement. And while I wasn't leading people into the promised land, my goal was similar…I wanted the kids to embrace the gift of a Catholic education given by their parents.

I squared my shoulders and read verse 8: "Don't be afraid, for the Lord will go before you and will be with you; he will not fail nor forsake you."

The teacher waved.

Strengthened, I entered the classroom, glanced at the crucifix, and began my story.

A mysterious illness had rendered me too weak to function. For months I couldn't drive my children to school, attend their sports events or volunteer in the classroom. Since, years earlier, I'd been diagnosed with a dormant cancer, my oncologist got involved.

"I believe this is the cancer," he said.

Sara's classmates prayed for me.

The night before learning the test results, I opened my Bible and read: "I will praise the Lord no matter what happens. I will constantly speak of his glories and grace." (Psalm 34:1)

I cringed, knowing the next day I might begin battling the dread disease that claimed the lives of both my parents. Would I be able to praise God 'no matter what'?

With that, an unexpected inner strength immediately arose, accompanied by an unworldly peace. Undoubtedly, I knew the power to give praise would persist.

Sara's classmates listened, all eyes on me.

"We have a God we can trust in all circumstances, to the grave and beyond," I advised. "There is no doubt about that."

The illness, which wasn't the cancer, ran a course. Good health returned.

Concluding, I urged the students to be thankful for the Catholic beliefs handed to them.

"Keep the faith," I said. "You will find it is the most important facet of your life. Keep it, not because it will make you healthy or give you what you want all the time, but because it will give you great peace."

It was an attentive audience. Nobody interrupted. Nobody smirked.

Instead, the kids sensed the power of my experience. They grasped the importance of faith.

The Black Leotard

When our daughters attended St. Mary Magdalen School, they knew I loved discussing the homilies delivered at the children's Masses. So, it didn't surprise me when, one day in December, Jenna, then 8, lingered in the kitchen to share the latest sermon.

"We went to church today," she said, waiting for me to set the mail aside. "Father Charlie suggested that for Advent we give up something really important to us, to make room for Christ in our lives."

She paused, then continued. "He said it could be something you own, like a favorite toy, or it could be something else…like you could give up your anger to forgive someone, or give up your time to help somebody, or something like that."

She glanced across the room to assure her sisters, Lynn, 12, and Sara, 5, weren't nearby.

"I know what I'm going to do," she said, stepping closer. Her eyes widened with excitement. Pulling my shoulder down to her level, she whispered, "I'm going to give Sara my black leotard."

My head spun. My heart stopped. I was speechless. *Had I heard right? The black leotard?* The same outfit she nearly ripped off Sara when she pranced around the house in it? The same outfit that caused our gentle Jenna to screech every time Sara 'borrowed' it? The same outfit that waged 'war' between the two?

Jenna would share *anything* with her kid sister, including her pony collection, Easy Bake oven, and her pink two-wheeler…but not that black leotard…And, of course, nothing attracted Sara more.

After insisting I heard correctly, Jenna skipped away in search of a box and gift wrap. I forgot about the conversation until after supper, when Jenna made an announcement.

"Sara, I have something to give you," she said. She raced to her bedroom and emerged with a brightly wrapped present, complete with a bow. "Here," she said. Smiling, Jenna handed over the box. "This is for you."

Sara cheerfully accepted the unexpected gift. When she spotted the prized leotard, she gasped. "This is for me?" she asked.

Jenna replied without hesitation. "Yep, it's yours."

Jenna beamed. Sara danced. They hugged. We laughed. It was hard to tell who was happier, the giver, the receiver, or us innocent bystanders.

Motivated by Jenna's sacrifice, I slipped away from the table and retrieved the emerald ring Lynn always wanted, but everyone knew I refused share it with her. It was authentic, I reasoned, and she might lose it.

Upon my return, I handed the ring to Lynn. "Here," I said. "This is for you."

Neither Jenna nor I ever looked back. We relinquished precious possessions, only to be filled with something greater. Jenna and Sara never fought about the leotard again. I don't know if Lynn still has the ring or not, but it doesn't matter. In giving something up, we received something better, something we never envisioned. We received freedom, peace, love, and forgiveness. We received the King of kings.

The Guest Speaker

When our church's Mothers' Group asked me to be a guest speaker, I jumped at the chance. I love to share my faith. And I love being a mother. I was thrilled for the opportunity. But at the same time, I was scared.

I'm a perfectionist. For weeks I scrawled notes while waiting in carpool lines, cooking dinner or watching television. Days before the talk, however, I still hadn't perfected my presentation. Worse yet, distractions abounded. Deadlines loomed. Our roof sprung a leak. The car broke down.

Finally, the night before my speech, I made a simple plan. My goal was to illustrate the importance of faith in a young child's life.

I pulled a picture of the Blessed Mother from our teenage daughter's bedroom. We had given it to her for her 8th birthday, along with an Easy Bake oven, a pink 'Skip-It', and a plush teddy bear. Her thank you note, handwritten in chunky second-grade print, read, "Dear Mom and Dad; Thank you for my birthday presents. I liked the Mary picture best." I made copies of it for handouts, hoping to illustrate how kids appreciate holiness.

I arrived early for the meeting. As we gathered, I prayed for these holy women of faith. With three nearly grown daughters, I understood the magnitude of their humble work. I felt honored to be in their presence. We formed a circle and prayed. Then, sitting beside them, I leaned forward and spoke.

I recalled the joys of chasing shadows with my toddler in the late afternoon sun. I recollected the power of three Hail Mary's and the peace they delivered as my brother lay dying twenty days after our youngest was born. I remembered transforming a boring day into lifetime memories when my two preschoolers and I strolled to the grocery store and bought an éclair to share on the way home. I recalled the nagging inner voice that convinced me to become a Brownie leader when I didn't really want to, and the incredible support the commitment provided at a time I needed it most.

I forgot about the Mary picture. I never distributed the handouts. I barely glanced at my outline. I engaged with the moms. At the conclusion, everyone graciously thanked me.

Later, however, I struggled. What if I bored them? How could I have abandoned my plan? Why did I forget the handouts? I chastised myself for not being more professional, informative, or organized. Then another realization surfaced.

God doesn't want our perfection, he wants our faithfulness.

With that, I found peace. I fulfilled the invitation to speak. My mission was complete.

You have a task, too. Don't be afraid to offer what you have. Your gift is important. It may not be much; it may be flawed. God will take the five loaves and two fish and multiply it. You may be a stuttering Moses or an aged Sarah, but He will work wonders with a willing heart.

After all, it's not all about us. It's all about Him.

Who Knew We Couldn't Wait to Visit Dad?

"I don't know why, but I have to go, and I have to go now," I said. My husband, just home from work, was clinking coins from his pockets into a green ceramic dish on our dresser as we discussed my idea of taking the kids on a road trip to visit my dad. At the time, I didn't realize how profound my words were.

The thought of traveling surfaced weeks earlier, but I resisted it. After all, my husband had to work and couldn't go with us. I was afraid to travel alone with the kids, both on the road and in hotels. I dreaded being trapped in a mini-van with three squabbling siblings. My husband, also anxious about our safety, couldn't understand why I wouldn't wait for a later date.

While a part of me hesitated, I knew that if I didn't visit Dad now, it would be another year before we'd be able to make the trip. With the kids out of school, summer was the perfect time to go. Despite my concerns, something wouldn't let me shake the thought of traveling to see Dad immediately.

Still, my own words surprised me: "I don't know why, but I have to go, and I have to go now." They were delivered with such authority that my husband and I ended our discussion. We called Dad, charted maps, made hotel reservations, and serviced the mini-van.

I'll never forget that moment, or the subsequent trip.

We visited Dad at his summer home in the mountains of upstate New York, where the acreage was lush, relaxing, and spacious. The kids laughed and giggled as Dad pulled them in a trailer attached to his ride-on mower. They roasted marshmallows on an open fire and feasted on gooey s'mores. He brought the kids shopping and they bought stuffed Dalmations and battery-operated horses that galloped and whinnied.

That Christmas, Dad planned to come to visit us in Florida, but he didn't. Health concerns kept him away. A cancer diagnosis followed, and the following spring, Dad passed away.

Had I waited another summer, the opportunity would have been gone.

Beneath my fears, despite my concerns, I believe it was God who prompted me to take that trip. When my husband and I discussed the pros and cons of travel that decisive afternoon, God spoke to me and through me.

Since then, whenever a nagging inner voice insists I do something, I respond. Not quickly, not impulsively, but I listen, over time; days, maybe weeks, to be sure it's a call from heaven itself. The prompting may not make sense, but it always persists. And, again and again, I've been amazed at the wonders of His touch.

The Prayer of a Summer Vacation

I clenched the steering wheel, watching the red lights of the traffic ahead of me through the blinding rain. Suddenly I wondered why a spontaneous road trip with the kids while my husband was away on business sounded like a good idea.

Halfway there, I realized I'd made a mistake.

The interstate became treacherous when a thunderstorm roared. Sheets of water covered our windshield faster than the wipers could clear it. Traffic slowed. I panicked, realizing we'd arrive at our destination—a remote cabin in the woods—long after dark.

My fears escalated. *Why did I insist on this trip? Why hadn't I listened to my husband's concerns? What if we had an accident? Would he forgive me?*

I wanted to go back home, but slippery roads made the trip uncertain in either direction. My adventurous spirit had us perched on a limb. Suddenly, I felt lonely, homesick and scared.

When we stopped for gas, I burst into tears. My kids sympathized, but Jenna, 13, encouraged me. "Mom," she said. "You've lost sight of the goal. Think about the mountains. Think about the horseback riding and whitewater rafting...Paint a picture..."

We forged ahead, arriving at our destination at twilight. The "town" was a single convenience store in the middle of nowhere. The cabin had no telephone, television or cellphone service.

Right or wrong, we were here. I had to make the best of it.

In the days that followed, calamity reigned. We locked our keys in the car, nearly descended a turbulent waterfall, and got lost searching for a Catholic church.

Inexplicably, however, help arrived. A locksmith appeared and unlocked our car. Something prompted us to exit the river before the hidden fall, and somehow, we located the church before Mass began.

We accomplished our goals, going whitewater rafting, horseback riding and hiking, but I couldn't wait for the trip to end.

When I was finally reunited with my husband, I sighed with relief as he wrapped his arms around me. I needed his embrace. I was glad to be home, where I knew I was safe.

Dear Lord, I learned so much this trip.

When we are lost, lonely, homesick--when life throws us a spontaneous curve and we want to go back, but we can't--when the way ahead feels uncertain and scary--when we're out on a limb just a little too far; remind us that there is no place too far from you.

Remind us that you are our goal, and that you are here for us, in every breath we take. Remind us that you will help us paint that picture, refresh that goal. Indeed the very hairs of our heads are numbered.

Show us, once again, the power of your quiet love. Show us that you go before us always, sending us helps and prompts. Remind us that even if we get a bit too independent from you, stray into our will and perhaps a bit out of yours, that your forgiveness awaits us with strong loving arms.

And thank you, Lord, for this adventure we call life.

Balance Beam Wonders

Parents, let your children make decisions. Sometimes, even when it doesn't appear to be that way, you'll be allowing God to work through them.

Like the time our teenage daughter Sara, a former competitive gymnast, agreed to give away the dusty balance beam occupying space in our garage. She wanted it to go to a good home—a girl who loved gymnastics like she once did. Callers flooded our answering machine as soon as I ran the ad for the free beam.

I returned the first call and advised they could have it. In the conversation, however, I discovered they wanted it for their karate school.

Sara was disappointed. "It needs to go a gymnast…." I agreed, but I had already promised it to the school.

However, the beam sat in our garage for weeks as the karate school owner searched for a truck to pick it up. In the meantime, our voice mail recorded countless calls. One in particular stayed with me.

"This is Stacy. My son had a stroke as an infant and now he needs to work on his balance. Your balance beam

could change his life, so if you haven't given it away yet, we would love to have it."

Even though it was promised to the karate school, I kept Stacy's name and number. Sara still insisted we find a young gymnast for the beam.

Then one night when I arrived home, Sara greeted me at the door. "Mommy, a girl named Lacy called about the beam. She's eleven years old and in gymnastics! I spoke with her dad too! This is really important to them! I want to give it to her," she pleaded.

We talked. The karate school decided they didn't want the beam. Sara knew that I wanted to help the woman with the toddler experiencing balance problems.

Although she felt compassion for him, Sara understood the thrill of back walkovers, handsprings and jumps on the beam. She recognized those needs in a way I never will.

Tears filled her eyes as I left the final decision to her. Finally, Sara said, "Let's call the girl's dad back."

We did and they happily made arrangements to pick up the beam the next day.

During our conversation, however, the dad mentioned that they too had a balance beam. It was too low to the ground and too short to accomplish complex gymnastics moves. They now planned to give it away.

I told them about Stacy, the mom of the boy who had the stroke, and put them in touch with each other.

About an hour later, Stacy called. "Thank you so much for remembering us," she said. "You didn't even know us, and I can't believe you kept our name and number! This lower beam will be better than yours would have been for my son. Look at how God provides. Thank you!"

Look at how God provides. I feared I wasn't teaching my daughter compassion in allowing her to choose who to give the beam to. Instead, we both learned something about the awesome providence of God.

Be careful what you pray for....

I'm not the kind to pray for a specific outcome. Instead, I pray for the gifts of the spirit: wisdom, understanding, courage, right judgment, knowledge, reverence and awe. I figure, who am I to dare tell God what to do?

But on this particular day, when Sara and I were visiting colleges, I broke the mold: I prayed for a parking space when we arrived at the university.

With 40,000 students and 10,000 parking spaces, I figured I needed divine intervention. Sure enough, we circled the congested parking lots only to find them crammed, until finally, among the last crowded rows, there was one narrow parking spot available.

"Take it!" Sara shouted.

I paused, surveying the space.

"I can't fit in there," I said.

"Yes, you can," she said. "Just try!"

The lot, designed for petite Volkswagen beetles, was overcrowded. An enormous sport utility vehicle filled the space to my left. A shiny long green metallic pickup truck occupied the spot to my right. The thought of squeezing my mini-van into the narrow sleeve between the two didn't equate.

But Sara urged me, and I didn't want to park miles away and hike in high heels, so I decided to have a crack at it.

I swung wide and aimed for center space. Halfway in, my left headlight nearly shaved the SUV beside us. On my right, you could floss between the rear corner of the green pickup truck and the side of my gray minivan.

My heart raced. My palms turned sweaty. I sucked in my gut, as if it could help.

Then a young man arrived. He threw his palms over his face as he watched the short erratic movements of my van, wedged between the SUV and the pickup.

I rolled my window down. "Is this your pickup?" I shouted.

He nodded and proceeded to guide me, as I inched to and fro until the van was finally sandwiched between the two vehicles.

Visibly shaken, I backed it up again, and centered it as best I could into the tiny space.

"Thank you for your help," I told the owner of the green pickup, who was just as relieved as me when I finally exited my vehicle.

"When are you leaving?" I asked him.

"In about an hour," came the reply.

"I hope your truck is gone by the time I have to leave," I said. I think he felt the same.

As Sara and I walked away, I looked at her. "Next time I'm going to pray for a parking spot that's easy to get into," I said, with a chuckle.

When our meeting ended, the truck was gone and the space remained empty, making an uncomplicated exit. It was another answer to prayer.

Honestly, though, next time I'll leave the circumstances to God.

Instead, I'll keep praying for courage, strength, wisdom and peace. After all, that's all I really needed to deal with the skinny parking space.

A Lesson in Divine Economy is Good for the Soul

I didn't want to help her. I really didn't.

I zipped into the parking lot of the new craft store. That's when I saw her.

The woman, with frizzy, shoulder-length hair, looked like a peasant wearing a long tiered, paisley skirt. She held a cardboard sign with big block letters containing the words "help" and "no work."

As I drove by, our eyes met.

Instinctively, I looked away.

I'm not going to stop, I thought. I don't have time. I don't have anything to give.

I drove to the furthest part of the parking lot and hurried into the store.

Once inside, I found the stationery I needed and purchased it with the promise that it could be returned if I found a better deal elsewhere.

Exiting, I glanced in the direction of the beggar, hoping she'd disappeared.

Unfortunately, she hadn't. She was still standing in the sweltering sun, holding her cardboard sign.

I hopped in my car and drove in the opposite direction. I'd nearly exited the lot when a nagging inner voice urged me to return.

I drove up to her and rolled my window down. The woman slowly stepped forward.

"What kind of help do you need," I asked.

"Money," she said. Despite her broken English, I learned the woman was from Guatemala and couldn't work because of a green card problem. Oddly, she also requested a gift card from the nearby grocery.

I can't afford that, I thought. I didn't have time for that. Instead, I handed her cash.

The woman accepted the money with a gracious smile. "Thank you," she said. She waved goodbye as I drove away.

That should have been it, but something told me to get her the gift card.

Really, I thought. Hadn't I already helped her? Why do more?

However, almost in a daze, I parked my car, entered the grocery and purchased a gift card. On the way out, I bought a chilled soda for her too.

Once outside, I delivered the gifts to the woman, who was still standing in the sweltering lot.

She thanked me and I left.

I never expected the gift to come back to me, but the unexpected happened later that afternoon when I found similar stationery for a lower price. I returned my original purchase and was heading to the cashier with the new boxes in hand when a fellow shopper stopped me.

"Do you want this coupon?" she asked. She thrust a piece of paper in my direction.

I accepted it, not realizing its value.

At the register, the calculations astounded me. The little coupon was priceless, producing a refund that exceeded my expectations. In fact, the final return amounted to more money than I'd given away.

I've always heard that God will not be outdone in generosity. Indeed, my gift to the Guatemalan woman had multiplied and returned in abundance…all in the same day.

And to think…I almost didn't help.

Leaping Lizards... How'd we get here??

I was glad my car was parked in the shade. The sun was hot, so it felt refreshing to slip into my vehicle, situated beneath a cluster of leafy shade trees. As I drove away, the lush landscape disappeared in my rearview mirror.

Moments later, I stopped at a red light. As I reached for the radio dial, I suddenly found myself face-to-face with a gaunt lizard clinging to my windshield wiper. Shrieking, I lurched backwards. Then, realizing the glass separated us, I relaxed.

Suddenly, the little chameleon was rather interesting.

I wondered why I hadn't noticed him sooner. We were about to turn onto a congested highway, surrounded by multiple lanes of concrete and a sea of steely automobiles. Not the environment for a reptile. I prayed the little guy would hang on.

As the light changed and traffic accelerated, the lizard, his long fingerlike feet clenched, clung to the wiper. His green skin was almost transparent, every muscle translucent. Motionless, he stared ahead. We sped along, but he never flinched.

Abruptly the traffic slowed to a crawl.

Don't jump now, I thought, hoping he wouldn't fall victim to the road. He rolled his big round eyes, but he didn't budge.

The smell of exhaust surrounded us. I feared for the safety of my newfound friend and wondered how I could save him from an ugly fate.

I considered turning my wipers on and flicking him to safety, but indeed, that would have only flung him into lanes of traffic. Not a good idea.

I thought about returning to the grassy parking lot, but that required intense maneuvering in this traffic.

"Hang in there," I mumbled. He turned his head in robotic movements, but otherwise, remained stationary.

We crept to the next intersection, where I exited the crowded highway. Traffic thinned. A canopy of oak trees lined the street and flourishing greenways wrapped around the little businesses. For the first time, the lizard inched forward.

"If you stay with me," I said aloud, "I'll drive you back to your parking lot!"

But before I could change direction, traffic stopped. This time the lizard leapt and disappeared. As traffic resumed, I searched for him, but he was gone.

I told the story to my friend Teresa.

"Life is like that," she said. "Sometimes our circumstances are scary and unfamiliar, and we don't know where we are going. We don't make a move.

Other times, we edge forward and survey the situation. Sometimes, it's time to make the leap."

We pondered how something as insignificant as a little lizard was capable of evaluating the bigger picture. What made him hang on? What made him know when it was okay to jump?

I still stand in awe.

We face challenging times and exciting times, quiet times and hectic times, times to lose and times to succeed. Imagine. If God can give this little creature such direction, think how much more he gives to you and me.

There is a right time for everything
– Ecclesiastes 3:1

Hovering Wings

I knew something was amiss when I arrived home to the sound of a helicopter hovering over our neighborhood. It hung in the air beating an ominous tune while I unloaded groceries from my car, put them away, and headed toward the computer.

I keep the books for my husband's business and I planned to enter a long list of invoices that afternoon. As usual, I checked my e-mails before starting, where a neighbor had issued a warning: *Residents: Lock your doors and stay inside. A gunman is loose in the area. Will keep you posted.*

I shook my head but felt strangely calm. Rather than fear my own safety, my thoughts turned to the distraught gunman. *How desperate he must be,* I thought, *to resort to hiding behind the barrel of a gun.*

With that, I began the tedious task of inputting vendors, dates, dollar amounts, and purchase order numbers. As each invoice was completed, I checked it off and moved on to the next.

About an hour later, with the helicopter still beating incessantly, another email appeared. *The gunman is holed up in an apartment nearby,* it said. *Swat teams are at a standoff with him.*

A wave of compassion swept over me.

How desperate, how alone and afraid, small and powerless he must feel, I thought. *And as horrible as his life must seem now,* I reasoned, *it most likely was about to get worse.* I whispered a prayer for the desperate gunman and proceeded to enter the next invoice.

Helicopter wings pounded overhead as the urge to pray grew into outright compulsion. Something was pushing me to pray and trying to ignore it was like trying not to blink for thirty minutes. I couldn't disregard it. It was uncontrollable. It had to happen.

Suddenly, I jumped from the computer and raced to a picture of Jesus in the Garden of Gethsemane that hangs in my bedroom. There, I dropped to my knees.

The prayers gushed forth.

I prayed for the gunman. I prayed his fear would subside. I prayed he wouldn't complicate matters by harming others. I prayed Jesus would intervene. I prayed for a peaceful resolution. I prayed for the stranger's conversion.

There, on my knees, an intense litany surged forth for this unknown gunman. Finally, after about 20 minutes, I relaxed. The prayer was done. I stood, looked at the picture of Jesus. *He's in your hands,* I said.

I returned to my desk and finished invoicing.

The helicopter still hovered when my husband and I went out to dinner that night, but when we returned, the skies were silent.

The next morning, I searched the newspaper for information on the incident before finding a brief article: *Altamonte gunman surrenders,* it said, *after holding police and swat teams at bay for over seven hours. He submitted peacefully at 7:40 pm. No shots were fired. Nobody was hurt.*

Try it...Will you let God bless you?

As I got dressed for work, the morning news delivered yet another round of massive layoffs, climbing unemployment rates, and Wall Street fraud. Suddenly, I realized I was holding my breath as concerns for my own financial security arose.

My head started spinning. *What will happen to my husband's business,* I wondered. *Nobody is buying expensive soup tureens in this economy.* My mind raced. *What will happen with my job?* The insurance business, somewhat insulated from simple fiscal downturns, was also feeling the effects of the eroding economic system.

Images of Wall Street flashed across the television as a reporter evaluated the proposed economic stimulus package. Another anchor warned viewers not to expect much from the new administration, while financiers agreed that our nation would feel the effects of the recession for a long time.

As I slipped into my shoes, my fears escalated. *What if we couldn't afford to repair the car? What if we had to bring our daughter back from college? What if the roof sprung a leak?*

The chattering telecast faded into the background, however, as a powerful conviction arose within me.

My God is bigger than Wall Street, I thought. *I'm not depending on an economic stimulus package, a president, an administration.*

I paused for a moment and glanced at the sky. *My God is bigger than all that.*

Along with the belief, an all-encompassing peace settled over me.

As I hopped into the car and drove to work, the local Christian radio program was urging listeners to support the station. It was the final day of Share-a-thon 2009, and they were 89% of their way to the goal.

I always listen to this radio station. For me, it's a form of prayer. I had considered donating days ago, but hesitated. After all, I reasoned, we needed to save our limited resources.

But today was the last day of the campaign, and with my newfound confidence, I realized that those of us who still had jobs and were able to pay our bills needed to help those who couldn't. And in these challenging times, this radio ministry is important.

I picked up my cellphone, dialed the station, and made a generous contribution.

Driving home later that day, however, fear crept in. *What had I done? What if we were to need that money? I should have stashed it away. Whatever possessed me to make that donation?*

I arrived home, kicked off my shoes, fed the cat, and checked my email. There, sitting in my inbox, precise, clear and exact, was an unexpected request from an editor offering me an attractive writing assignment. Not only was the project one I'd relish, but the pay was enough to cover my donation with lots of money to spare.

Bring all the tithes into the storehouse so that there will be food enough in my temple; if you do, I will open up the windows of heaven for you and pour out a blessing so great you won't have room enough to take it in! Try it! Let me prove it to you!" **Malachi 3:10**

Why Doesn't Somebody Help?

Sitting in traffic, I tapped my fingers on the steering wheel and glanced at the clock. If only this logjam would loosen, I'd get to church on time.

As usual, I was starting my workday with Mass.

"What's the holdup," I wondered, straining to look beyond the string of crawling traffic. Finally, I spotted the culprit—a sedan at the side of the road with a raised hood. A young, brown-haired woman stared helplessly at the engine.

I sat in line, watching the minutes tick away, fearing this delay would make me late to Mass. I watched as multiple drivers passed slowly by her without offering assistance. I shook my head. *Why didn't someone help her?* How frustrating. Someone ought to help. Not me, though. How could I? I didn't know her. I couldn't fix cars. I couldn't be late to my destination.

As I approached the stranded motorist, I looked away. I hugged the bumper of the car in front of me, and crept by, finally leaving the marooned driver in my rearview mirror.

Only then did I realize I was the one who had to help! I didn't have much to offer, but I had to do something! It didn't matter if I was late to church. If I didn't help her, I was missing the whole point.

I made a u-turn, re-entered the congested intersection, and crawled my way back to the abandoned driver. It took several minutes. I prayed the whole way that someone else would have helped her by the time I arrived so I could make it to church on time.

But no one did.

I parked nearby. "What's wrong?" I called.

Relief washed over her face.

"I don't know," she said. "My car just died. Sometimes I can get it to start again, but not this time."

"How can I help?" I asked.

"I need to get to my class," she said. "Could you drive me there? I can take care of the car later."

Surprisingly, her destination happened to be across the street from my church.

"Hop in," I said, as she grabbed her books and purse.

We introduced ourselves and I learned that Emma was studying to be a medical technician. She wanted to help others and was excited about her future. I encouraged her in her goals. As we spoke, a deep connection formed.

When we arrived at the school, Emma thanked me for the ride. I'll never forget her parting words: "We'll meet again."

Her statement startled me. I'll never recognize her again, but I knew she was right. Although I may not meet Emma personally, she'll be in the medical technicians I'll encounter throughout my life. She'll be in the young adults I meet seeking direction and guidance. She'll be in the stranger who needs my assistance.

I waved goodbye, drove across the street, parked my car, and raced into church, fully expecting to be late for Mass. However, as I took my seat, the priest was just walking down the aisle. Surprisingly, I didn't even miss the opening prayer.

Amazing, isn't it?

Our God really is an awesome God.

Angels in Disguise

Sometimes we wonder why we do the things we do. Sometimes, we find out.

Like the Saturday night I decided to get a haircut. Saturdays are typically 'date night' for my husband and me, so it broke routine. But something nagged me to get a haircut that day. Late afternoon, I finally succumbed and dialed the salon.

"They're probably closed," I thought. But the receptionist said they could take me if I came right away….

Simultaneously, a hefty woman, with unkempt, dark curly hair, stepped outside her tenement, looked to the heavens and heaved a great sigh. She began shifting one foot in front of the other, laboring her way past sub-shops, clothing stores and restaurants. Cars, trucks and busses dashed by, oblivious to the lone, lumbering figure. When she finally stopped to rest at a roadside bench, shoppers zipped by without a smile or kind word.

Odd, what she needed the most surrounded her, but she had no way to get it. She was hungry, but she had no food. There was a grocery, but she had no money. She'd walked a long way from home, but she didn't have the strength to return.

Finally, dejected and weary, she sat on a bench outside the salon, placed her head in her hands and surrendered to the tears. "Please Jesus," she prayed, "Please send someone to help me."

I pulled my van alongside the curb, threw the gearshift in park, exited, and raced inside the salon. In passing, I spotted the woman sitting on the bench, but I dismissed her.

My stylist scrubbed my hair and clipped the strands, rattling incessantly about a recent movie she saw. When I finally left, the first brushes of nighttime blanketed the street.

I fetched my keys and stepped off the curb when someone approached. It was the hefty woman with shabby, dark curly hair.

"Excuse me, ma'am," she said, stepping into the light. "Can you help me?"

I bristled, but something told me not to worry.

"What do you need?" I asked.

"I don't have any food," she said. As she explained her plight, I knew I could help.

"Hop in the car," I said. "We can go to the grocery store across the street."

"I knew God would send someone to help me," she said, climbing into my van. "And when I saw you walking into the hair-cutting place, I knew you were my angel."

She told me she became a Christian as a teen, and that God always met her needs in desperate situations, like this one. She admitted she didn't really know where she was going when she started walking that evening and I confessed the salon wasn't my normal Saturday night stop.

As our stories unraveled, I sensed her faith. Indeed, it was a privilege to help her. I'll forever remember our encounter, her devotion, and the wonder of a God who brought us together.

Don't forget to be kind to strangers, for some who have done this have entertained angels without even realizing it. (Hebrews 13:2)

Want to make a little change for the New Year?

I rummaged through my desk, searching for the annual pledge card our parish mailed to us. For weeks I delayed returning it, trying to ignore the small inner voice urging me to increase our monthly contribution, but the deadline was now.

I never doubted that my husband and I would match our expiring pledge, but I struggled with the relentless idea that we should increase the amount.

The timing couldn't have been worse.

We'd just taken on a car loan, our insurance rates doubled, and a recent hospital stay delivered a big unexpected bill. Additionally, television news blasted reports of America's looming financial cliff, which would leave us with increased taxes and smaller paychecks.

Why would we increase our tithe at a time like this?

I found the pledge card in a stack of papers and reviewed the giving guide, containing suggested amounts to make one small step in financial commitment to the church. I studied the numbers, folded the brochure in my hands, and listened again to the still small voice urging me to make the leap. Finally, I completed it, committing to the increased amount.

Then I drove to the church, pledge card in hand. As I arrived, I phoned my husband, hoping he'd talk me out of the increased commitment. However, when he suggested we maintain the status quo, wait to increase our pledge, or offer a smaller upturn, I became convinced we needed to make the step of faith now.

"You know God won't let us drop," I finally said. "I just feel like we are being called to do this. There's always a reason. God will not be outdone in generosity."

I hung up, entered the church, and delivered our pledge card. The commitment was made. The increase wasn't a large amount, but it was a giant leap for us.

Later that afternoon, an endorsement to our insurance policy arrived in the mail. Although it had accomplished the requested change, something didn't look quite right, so I emailed Scott, our agent.

Minutes later, he responded with an answer I never expected.

"This is to confirm I have corrected the endorsement to your insurance policy," Scott's email read. He proceeded to advise that we'd get money back and defined the exact annual amount.

I gasped, punching a few numbers into the calculator. What was the yearly increase in our pledge?

Indeed, as the calculations appeared, they confirmed my suspicions. The increase in our pledge was offset by the unexpected refund. In fact, the refund was larger, leaving us with lots of change in our pockets.

When you help the poor, you are tending to the Lord-and he pays wonderful interest on your loan! Proverbs 20:17

What Was I Thinking?

Before I opened my eyes for the day, I felt burdened. My mind raced, swirling with fears for both now and the future.

Yesterday's optometrist's appointment shattered my childlike expectation that my eyesight would always be fixable. A drastic change in prescription…was than an area of double vision? Now we need computer glasses in addition to trifocals? And some tests?

My thoughts galloped into the future. What if I slowly went blind? What if I couldn't work? Worse yet, what if I couldn't write?

Additionally, immediate concerns invaded my thoughts. I faced urgent deadlines at the office that day. One project had to be completed and handed off before noon. Another, requiring extensive research was due at the end of the day. Yet another complicated submission was waiting in the wings. How would I handle the demands? Would it get done? Would I have to work late?

After all, there never seemed to be enough time. My husband and I wanted to visit my in-laws, who were struggling with health issues. We wanted to enjoy the grandchildren, attend their soccer games and dance recitals, to have them spend the night and go to Steak N' Shake. And how about making a meal for the neighbor who was just diagnosed with cancer?

Finally, I opened my eyes. It was time to get to Mass. I threw on clothes and headed to church.

Streams of morning light spilled across the landscape as I pulled into the parish parking lot. A cool breeze caressed my face as I raced toward the church.

Inside, I took my place in the pew, knelt down and prayed.

As I bowed my head, fears about my eyesight, concerns about the day's demands, and struggles about finding time for others surfaced.

Unexpectedly, in the silence, an answer arose. It came without asking. It arrived without effort. The words were distinct and clear. They were for me and they were for you.

"Don't think about what you can't do…think about what you can do," I heard.

Immediately the burden lifted. My mind flooded with thoughts of all I could do, even if I lost my sight.

I could think. I could talk. I could hug. I could love. I could smell, taste, and hear. I could eat. I could pray. I could be.

A wave of peace washed over me.

Later that day, as I handled my work, I focused on the file in my hands instead of stressing about the looming deadlines awaiting my attention. With each assignment, I realized what I could do for that project, completed it, and then moved on to the next. It was very peaceful.

As for the family...we went to the soccer game. We visited the in-laws. Rather than focus on what still needed to be done, I gave those precious moments my undivided attention.

And peace reigns. The advice was simple. It was divine. It was worth sharing.

Don't think about what you can't do...think about what you can do.

When something seems like forever...maybe it's not!

Young kids can surprise us with the things they say. Sometimes as in this case, they deliver a divine perspective.

It all began when I told a story about my mother. Avé, my five-year-old granddaughter, cocked her head. "Your mother," she asked, "Who is she?"

"Oh, you don't know her," I replied, with a wave of my hand. "She died before you were born."

I looked away, thinking the conversation had ended.

But as an afterthought, I mumbled, "In fact, she died before your mother was born."

Moments later, I heard her tiny voice fumbling with the words. "She died? W-where is she?"

Before I could respond, Avé spoke again. "Is she in heaven?"

Relief washed over me. Avé could understand that. Sadly, she was introduced to the concepts of death and heaven after my daughter gave birth to a stillborn last year.

"Yes," I said, sitting back in my chair. "Yes, she's in heaven."

My little granddaughter looked up. Our eyes met in one intense moment.

"Still?" she asked. "She's in heaven…Still?"

I chuckled at her comment until, days later, I found myself struggling with an ethical issue.

Unexpectedly, I was in a whistleblower-type situation at work where I was the one who would have been making the noise. It happened when I was directed to send an email with a slanted reply to keep a transaction alive. When I questioned this, I was told that the partial answer "wasn't a big deal."

Of course, it was. Most likely the contract would cancel if all the details were disclosed.

Struggling, I hesitated to send the skewed communication.

"Why are you making such a big deal," my coworker finally grumbled. "Do you want to rock the boat? This is a done deal. Just answer the way I told you. Otherwise, you might create problems."

I didn't want to instigate difficulties. I didn't want to disrupt relationships. It wasn't my fault anyway, was it? Someone else was telling me what to say, right? Still grappling, I pushed the send button.

But the knot in my stomach didn't disappear like the words on the computer screen.

Rather, the agony escalated. I woke up in the dark of the night, wrestling with my decision. Tossing and turning, I realized there was no easy solution.

My Emmaus Walk

The next morning, I dreaded powering up my computer.

I couldn't escape the anxiety. I suffered for what seemed an eternity and then, while praying for guidance, I suddenly remembered the message delivered by my granddaughter: This life is not forever. Eternity lasts an eternity.

Had my perspectives been upside down? Was I more concerned about easing the discomfort of this temporal life than in its everlasting consequences?

With that, I felt courageous.

Bracing myself, I sent a corrected email, adding the details previously omitted. I didn't know what would happen, but I prayed for strength to deal with the aftermath.

Instead, chaos never came. Finally, after what seemed an eternity but in reality was less than 24 hours, the responding email arrived.

"Not a problem," it read. "Proceed as planned."

Dear God, what's in a name?

The Lord's voice is typically subtle, but he's always there...even in the small stuff. Every detail matters. Nothing is too insignificant for him.

I was reminded of that recently, when, on an uneventful weekday morning, I found myself pondering our youngest grandson's name.

Seriously, I don't know what made me wonder about Dominic's name that particular day, but I kept thinking about it as I got ready for Mass. And I couldn't quit.

After all, there's a definite pattern to his siblings' names, but his name, Dominic, is clearly out-of-sync.

Let me explain: There are the girls, named Avé, Angelina, Abigail (stillborn) and Ayla. All their names begin with an 'a'. It's a nice, tight package.

And there are the boys, Matthew, James and Dominic. The first two sound like gospel writers, right? Then we have Dominic….definitely not a gospel writer. Wouldn't Mark or John have been a better match? What about Luke or Paul?

Actually, this wasn't the first time I realized Dominic's name didn't follow suit. However, that particular day,

I couldn't shake the thought. I wondered…was it even a holy name?

Washing my face, I laughed at my silly ideas. After all, it was too late. Dominic was already a toddler. There was no changing his name.

But, brushing my hair, I continued to speculate, mouthing his name: Dominic. That name is so different, I thought. It wasn't a family name. Really, why Dominic? Where was the holiness?

Grabbing my keys, I drove along a shady, tree-lined street to church. Parking the car, I headed inside, forgetting about my earlier obsession with Dominic's name.

Little did I know, but God didn't forget. He had already prepared a message for me.

The priest approached the altar, stood at the ambo, and welcomed the congregation. Then, much to my surprise, he announced that today was the Feast of St. Dominic.

My head spun, remembering how, on that morning in particular, I'd been obsessed with my little grandson's name. I'd wondered why he didn't have a gospel writers' name like his brothers. I'd even questioned if his was a holy name.

Amazing, isn't it? What are the odds I would be wrestling with Dominic's name on the day that, unbeknownst to me, happened to be the Feast of St. Dominic?

The priest's homily was about St. Dominic, and his sermon seemed tailor-made for me. I learned the saint was a spirited evangelist.

Clearly God was happy with Dominic's name. It didn't have to be a gospel writers' name. It didn't have to be a family name. Rest assured, Dominic is a holy name.

When writing this column, I felt reluctant to share something as trivial as my grandson's name. But this story packs a powerful message.

It reminds us that our God is with us. He cares, he leads, he speaks, he guides. He knows our every thought. He knows when we sit and when we stand.

Indeed, he's interested in the smallest details of our lives.

After all, what's in a name?

What I learned from a kid's science lesson

"Grandma, grandma!"

Matthew, my 6-year-old grandson, shouted as he jumped out of the big white van, waving a florescent plastic star in his hand. Angelina, 5, emerged, brandishing pages of black construction paper covered with yellow circles. Avé, 7 at the time, followed, leaping from the vehicle wielding a Ziploc bag filled with black play dough that was covered in glitter.

"Group hug," I said, as they raced toward me. We embraced, wiggling in delight. "How was your class on outer space?"

The girls explained that the construction paper cutouts represented planets and the sparkly black play dough resembled moon rocks.

Finally Matthew spoke up.

"Grandma," he yelled. "Look at this!"

He held a plastic star in his hand, raising it for me to see.

"The teacher says it glows in the dark," he said. "We're going into Angelina's closet to see it. You want to come with us?"

"Sure," I shouted. "I love glow in the dark stuff!"

Immediately the small band of siblings dashed inside. Eyes shining with delight, they raced down the hallway to Angelina's room.

I caught their excitement. I caught their joy. I couldn't wait to see the star glow in the dark. I ran after them.

Once we reached Angelina's room, we piled into the closet and jammed the door shut. Everything went black.

We could no longer see the ruffled dresses hanging on the racks beside us. The pile of dirty clothes on the closet floor was no longer visible. Even the faces of my grandchildren disappeared in the dark.

Matthew thrust the star high above his head. It was easy to spot. There was no missing it. In fact, it was the only thing you could see, and it was glowing brightly through the gloom.

We turned to stare at it. There was silence, except for a chorus of oooh's and aaah's elicited by all of us. We were star-struck.

"Cool, isn't it?" Matthew asked.

Indeed it was. Indeed, it captivated us.

And I thought.

Sometimes we are in the dark.

It may be health concerns or grief issues. Maybe it's financial problems or difficult business decisions. Perhaps it's the challenges of friendships or married life.

In this life, darkness does exist.

That's when we need someone to show us the light. We need someone to invite us, to be so excited about this light that we race to follow.

That light, of course, is the light of Christ. That person, of course, is you and me.

We are the light of the world.

Years ago, when I was ill, my Bible-study group delivered meals. When I battled guilt after my brother's untimely death, a friend helped me accept the mercy of God. During the recent recession, an unexpected inheritance arrived from a faith-filled relative.

Those actions lit up my world and brought me to Christ.

Yes, we are the light of the world. Catch the excitement. Bring others along with you. And hold that Christ-light high.

You'll see. It'll glow in the dark.

What's the most embarrassing thing ever happened to you?

"Grandma, tell us a story!" My granddaughters bounced onto the sofa, eyes sparking with delight.

"I can't think of any," I said. "I've told you all my stories."

Avé, twisting her long, blond pigtails, spoke. "What was the most embarrassing thing that ever happened to you?"

Hands down, I had a story.

"Well, when I was in middle school, I went to the store with my friend, Madelyn," I said…

It was a small five-and-dime. We were browsing the toiletries aisle, where Madelyn was studying curlers and hair spray. As we discussed the products, I found myself squaring my shoulders. We were growing up, weren't we?

A few feet away, some sweet-smelling deodorant demanded attention. I didn't really wear deodorant yet, but some of my friends did. Maybe I should purchase some. Surely, it was the prestigious thing to do. It would elevate me in the sight of my peers, right?

My Emmaus Walk

I took another sniff, replaced the lid, and decided I had to have it. I fingered the cash in my pocket…my own money that I'd earned while babysitting. Wouldn't it be great to use my own money to buy something so grownup? The idea made me stand a little taller.

But I hesitated. I'd never bought deodorant before. I'd used my babysitting money to purchase music, candy, jump ropes and hula hoops, but never deodorant. The thought of buying something so personal made me nervous.

Then, I had an idea. "Madalyn," I said. She was, after all, my best friend.

Her long brown hair bounced on her shoulders as she turned my way. "Yes," she asked.

"I want this deodorant but I'm too embarrassed to buy it. Will you?"

Her eyes widened as she covered her mouth in a mock gasp.

"What?!" she said. "Why? Just buy it! What's to be embarrassed about?"

"No, yeah, I can't," I said. "I don't know. I can't do it. I'll give you the money. Will you just buy it for me?"

'Come on," she said. "Buy it yourself!"

But I insisted.

"I really can't…I don't know why, but it's embarrassing." I glanced around the little, quiet store with only a handful of customers. "What if someone sees me," I said. "Pleeeease."

"Okay," she said, grabbing the deodorant and the money.

I sighed with relief and followed her to the cashier.

Moments later, Madelyn paid for the deodorant. I watched the cashier bag the purchase and hand it to Madelyn, along with the change. With that, Madelyn turned to me, held the bag out, and, in a loud voice, announced, "Here's your deodorant, Debbie."

I nearly melted into the floor. My face reddened. I scurried to the exit, grumbling to Madelyn the whole way. (Yes, we remained friends.)

My granddaughters rolled in laughter. Me, too.

"I learned from that," I said. "I learned to have courage to do something I know I need to do. I learned to laugh at myself. I learned that truth will always be told, even if we try to hide it."

Life lessons for all of us.

God Loves You and So Do I

"God loves you and so do I."

That was Grandma Peg's tagline. She wrote it in every communication. I can still envision her cursive handwriting, complete with loops and scrolls.

"God loves you and so do I."

She penned that on birthday cards, holiday greetings, and gift tags. Once, when flowers arrived with a card that simply read, "God loves you and so do I," we knew Grandma Peg sent them.

Peg was my stepmother. She married Dad, who was widowed, when my husband and I were juggling our first baby. Instantly, Peg became grandma. Although we lived states away, she began teaching invaluable lessons.

Faith was our connection. We attended Mass and prayed together. But Grandma Peg brought holiness to a new level. She was the first person to 'pray over' me, although I nearly cringed at the thought. She introduced me to prayer meetings and charismatic music.

During our visits, I'd awake to find her sitting in a chair, reading her Bible and praying. That image was captivating. For those precious moments, she seemed to be in another world, a very peaceful place.

Once Grandma Peg and I were in the kitchen when she reached for something to write on, which happened to be a grocery receipt.

"Sometimes things just come to me," she said. She scribbled a few lines and handed it to me.

"My children," it said. "I bring you my love. Remain steadfast. Walk with me. Trust me. Obey me. Believe me. Love me. I am your Lord God."

Another time we were chatting when she arose, dug through her purse, wrote a check and handed it to me. I tried to resist but she insisted.

"I just felt like God was asking me to do that," she said.

I wonder if she knew the money was a lifeline at that particular time.

Dad died, but she remained a central figure in our lives. We continued to receive letters, flowers and cards from her with the enduring message, "God loves you and so do I." Eventually, I began writing it in my correspondences back to her.

In fact, I found myself following in her footsteps. I'd start my day reading the Bible and praying. When her health declined, I'd quote scripture to encourage her. In her darkest moments, I'd pray right over the phone with her.

Within hours of her death, I arranged flights and made plans to attend her funeral. Days later, I flew home and returned to work.

That's when the enormity of the loss hit. I felt overwhelmed by sadness. In my sorrow, I longed for a connection to her.

The afternoon passed slowly. At closing time, I wiped my tears and shut the computer down. As was our custom, I hugged my coworker Michelle goodbye.

As we embraced, Michelle, knowing I'd had a difficult day, spoke.

"I wanted to tell you something my mama always used to say," she said.

Then, unbeknownst to her, Michelle delivered a message straight from the heart of Grandma Peg. It was balm for my sorrowing soul.

"God loves you and so do I."

God's power--perfected in our weaknesses?

Sometimes our own character traits are a double-edged sword.

For instance, I'm flexible, so flexible, in fact, that I'm sometimes accused of being indecisive. Sometimes, like last Halloween, my dithering decisions rule.

My husband was out-of-town on business when Sara, our youngest daughter, drove home from cheerleading practice with a request.

"Can we go to Lynn's house for dinner?" she asked. Our oldest daughter had invited us.

I shifted my feet, unwilling to admit that I wanted to stay home and distribute candy.

"I don't know…." I said. "Do you want to?"

"Yes," Sara shot back. "I'll take a quick shower and we'll go."

"Okay," I said, halfheartedly.

I really wanted to stay home, visit my neighbors, admire the ballerinas and ghosts, and dispense candy. It was a tradition I treasured.

But I wanted to make my daughters happy, too.

Indecision reigned.

My Emmaus Walk

As Sara hopped in the shower, I dumped miniature chocolates and assorted lollipops into an oversized bowl and placed it on the doorstep. But as I scrawled a note suggesting trick-or-treaters help themselves to the sweets, I changed my mind.

"I'm not going," I announced when Sara emerged.

She urged me to go, but I explained my desire to personally deliver the treats.

"Okay," she said.

Moments later, Sara grabbed her car keys and headed to the garage. As the ignition roared, I changed my mind and signaled to her to wait for me. But as I flicked on the porch light and locked the front door, I wavered.

"Go ahead," I said. "I'm not going to go."

Sara sighed and I watched, somewhat wistfully, as her vehicle's taillights disappeared into the darkness.

I called Lynn to advise I wasn't coming. Then I hung up with a sense of regret and yet another decision—I would join them for dinner, after all!

As I settled in for the solitary drive, I phoned my longtime friend, Gloria. We chuckled about my nonsense, resulting in two cars traveling separately to the same destination, and me missing Halloween at my house as if it were a grave mistake.

Then Gloria, who was recently widowed, told me how happy she was that I phoned. She'd received a promotion at work that day and wanted to tell someone, but she didn't know who to call. Mourning the death of her husband, she felt her loss in a painful way when she couldn't share the news with him.

"Your call was like an answer to prayer," Gloria said. "It's like God used you to reach me at just the perfect moment, when I needed it most."

And I wonder…could our weaknesses play a role in God's greater plan?

After all, I wouldn't have phoned Gloria had I stayed home to distribute candy. I wouldn't have phoned her had I traveled with Sara.

It had to be as it was; a goofy, mixed-up, belated decision to go, resulting in my solo travel. And, unbeknownst to me, with exact timing, it prompted me to contact, of all people, my friend Gloria--right when she needed it most.

Each time he said, "…I am with you; that is all you need. My power shows up best in weak people." 2Cor 12:9

Let the Windfall Where It May

Nobody likes a bargain more than me.

So I was thrilled when the expenditures on our once-in-a-lifetime trip to Rome appeared to be under budget. But I struggled with the message that accompanied that realization.

Even while travelling, I noticed my husband and I weren't spending as much as we expected. The restaurants weren't pricey. Our hotel, despite a 3-star rating, was charming. We walked everywhere, eliminating the cost of public transportation.

So, even before heading home, I anticipated substantial savings.

We prayed in gratitude for the unexpected windfall, but whenever we did, something seemed to tell me that all the excess money wasn't ours to keep. Rather, we needed to share it.

Additionally, a particular coworker came to mind, along with a specific sum of money.

Back home, I waited for the bills to settle. Maybe international fees or conversion costs would consume the anticipated savings, but that didn't happen.

Instead, the feeling that I had to give that exact amount of money to that particular coworker persisted.

Amy, a middle-aged woman, was new to our office, but we'd had a conversation where I learned that both her parents died when she was young. I knew she believed in God and saw His miraculous work in her life.

Still, I barely knew her.

For weeks, I resisted. Why not keep the money? Or give her half the amount?

Obstacles arose. Would I give her cash? Nobody carries that amount of cash. Check? I disliked that thought.

Fears invaded. Would she think I was rich? Would she expect future loans?

However, the still, small voice persisted. It had to be that exact amount to that particular person.

Finally, I surrendered.

"God, if you want me to give her the money, I will," I prayed. "But you need to make a way."

That morning, our paths crossed. When Amy asked about my Italy trip, we agreed to meet in the lunchroom. I'd bring my pictures. As my story unfolded, I found myself telling her how the trip cost only half of what we'd budgeted for it.

As we parted, she mentioned that she was heading to the bank.

I knew this was an answer to prayer.

I hurried to my office, wrote the check and slipped it on her desk.

Moments later, she found me. Waving the check, she tried to return it.

"I can't keep this," she said.

I raised my hands, refusing the check. "It's yours," I said.

"Are you sure," she asked, incredulous.

"Yes, keep it."

"Thank you," she said.

"Don't thank me," I responded. "Thank God."

She nodded, tears in her eyes. "I do," she said. "But I thank you too."

Later, she confided that weeks ago she'd received an unexpected bill. The due date was approaching and she lacked funds to cover it. She began praying for a specific sum of money, even posting a check on her refrigerator indicating the amount needed. It was the exact amount I'd given her.

We're friends now but she's never asked to borrow a dime.

Rather, we stand in awe together, praising a God who hears our prayers and moves mountains to meet our every need.

Oh, Say, Can You See the Emerging Beauty?

I didn't really want to make the little cardboard houses.

I just wanted the glorious end result.

I'm housebound, recovering from cancer treatments, and I need goals. Praying is great. Writing is good. Reading is wonderful…but I need to accomplish something with my hands…something where I can see the end result… something tangible.

So…I remembered the little cardboard houses.

Years ago, when I was a Brownie leader, one of the moms made cardboard "gingerbread" houses for the girls to decorate. They were sturdy. They were big. The kids loved it and so did I.

I'm not crafty, but as my children grew, we shared the idea with their soccer teams, cheerleading teams, and neighbors. Someone else would make the cardboard houses and we'd gather at my home to decorate them. They brought such joy to everyone.

As the kids moved on with their lives, we stopped making them.

My Emmaus Walk

But now, with a need for a tangible goal and with lots of grandchildren as my audience, I decided to resurrect the tradition.

That meant I had to build the basic structures, and, oh, what a mess I am at that!

Anyway, armed with good reason, I mentally committed to making one house a month. That seemed doable. That felt realistic. And we'd have plenty ready to decorate during the holidays.

I dawdled in January, dreading the actual work of it. Crunch time…was I going to do this or not?

Finally, I dragged out the scissors, cardboard and tape. I eyeballed the cardboard, cut it, and tried to tape it together.

There were gaping holes. It was a little lopsided. The tape didn't stick very well.

But I persisted. I found better tape. I covered the gaps. I pushed the walls into place.

Finally, I held the finished craft at arm's length. Turning it slowly, I observed every angle. As I studied it, a smile formed on my lips.

I imagined one of my grandchildren selecting this particular house. I pictured her slathering icing over it and carefully choosing colorful candies to decorate it. I heard her laugh. I saw her smile.

I saw my grandson delivering a stunning creation to the residents at my mother-in-law's assisted living facility. I saw him walking through the doors, placing his masterpiece in the gathering room. I saw a slow smile spread across the face of a white-haired gentleman. I saw a woman pushing a walker stop and thank him for the beautiful gingerbread house.

Deep within, a sense of satisfaction arose.

As imperfect as the little cardboard house was, I found myself admiring it. I saw such beauty in it.

Suddenly I wondered: Is this how God sees us?

Sin destroyed his perfect creation. There's pride and self-centeredness. There's laziness and thoughtlessness. We're crooked, lopsided and unstable.

Maybe God holds us in the palm of his hand… he molds us and shapes us…providing direction here, pushing the walls in place there…

Maybe he sees beyond the mess. Maybe he envisions the ultimate beauty and unending joy we were designed to deliver…

And maybe, just maybe, he smiles.

He's Still the Reason for the Season

"I'm starting my Christmas shopping this weekend," I said to a coworker recently.

"So early?" she asked.

I nodded. "Last year the holidays were so stressful that I've decided to get the shopping done before Thanksgiving. That way there's time for church presentations and holiday gatherings."

"I don't know why we do this to ourselves," my associate said, shaking her head.

Before long, we found ourselves bemoaning the fact that Christmas had become too commercialized. Did people lose the real meaning of the season? Was it all about retail sales? Why create all this stress?

"I'd rather see people give gifts throughout the year, instead of just one day," she said. I nodded in absolute agreement.

That weekend, however, as I took my Christmas list to the stores, I changed my mind.

I realized a world without Christmas gift-giving would be very sad and cold, indeed.

Suppose there were no bell-ringers for the Salvation Army? Suppose you never heard Joy to the World piped though a retail outlet? Of if school choirs didn't visit the mall wishing us a Merry Christmas?

Suppose we weren't prompted to consider sharing our resources, like our food, our time and our gifts, in some way, with family, friends and neighbors. What would that look like?

For a season, the spirit of Christmas surrounds us. It's a spirit of love.

Some may measure the season by retailers' revenues, but it's far more than that.

It's about the incalculable amount of love that motivates those transactions. Without the love, there would be no inflated sales.

Should we eliminate the commercialism prompted by Christmas Day? Balance what we do throughout the year and eradicate the need to mark the occasion?

That would be like having someone's birthday pass without any special recognition. We treat you nicely all year long, so why celebrate?

Could we really refrain from that? I couldn't.

I want to celebrate you. I like to recognize birthdays….yours, mine….and Jesus'.

We can and should give of ourselves throughout the year. We can still be generous, create happy surprises, and make someone smile…any day of the year…every day of the year!

This, precisely, is what Christmas is all about.

And the commercialism?

Many of us don't sew, bake, hammer or build anything useful. Generations ago, you had to. Thankfully, times have changed.

Now we shop in malls. There's Amazon. We order online.

Why should Christmas be any different?

However, it's not about overspending. A note and a candy bar can be the sweetest gift. In God's economy, a smile, a hug, a visit or a silent prayer are priceless presents.

So let the retail ratings soar.

But don't forget why.

Don't forget the love of God poured out on us this Christmas Day. Ponder the birth of the One sent to open the doors of heaven to you for eternity.

That's the gift we celebrate on Christmas Day. And this gift is never-ending. The love of God pursues you today and all the days of your life.

You can be sure of that.

You can celebrate that.

Today and every day.

Welcome to the New Year... Are you singing a new song?

Play joyous melodies of praise upon the lyre and on the harp. Compose new songs of praise to him, accompanied skillfully on the harp; sing joyfully. Psalm 33: 2-3

With the rush of the holidays behind us, I've taken down the Christmas tree, bundled the lights, and packed the nativity, snow globes and wreaths into the garage. I love turning the page on the calendar. The New Year is time for a new beginning, a letting go of the past, a fresh look at tomorrow.

But change is difficult and starting something new requires effort.

For instance, I recall the music lessons from my childhood. I couldn't wait to learn how to play the accordion. Anyone who has ever played an instrument knows that learning how to read music, handle the instrument and get it to emit any kind of noise are achievements in themselves. Those first erratic chords are a major accomplishment. It takes hours and hours of practice before the first sounds of a melody emerge. Nobody can just pick up an instrument and play a beautiful tune. We work up to it.

Singing a new song to the Lord is similar. New beginnings may fluster us and cause us to question if we will ever be comfortable again. Our bumpy starts do not indicate failure, simply a need to persevere until we are skillfully playing. Initially, we may not be harmonious, but with practice and dedication, a melodious composure will result.

Several years ago, I made the biggest New Year's resolution of my life. Following the call to write, I abandoned former responsibilities in the workplace to pursue a career in publishing. I traded proficiency in the insurance business for inexperience as a writer, cherished co-workers for a blank computer screen, and a bustling downtown commute for a solitary home office. The transition was long and lonely. In the beginning, nothing was harmonious.

Then Together in Christ published a meditation I wrote. The Word Among Us accepted my parenting articles. Upper Room, On Mission magazine and Lifestyle publications printed my work. The Florida Catholic invited me to write this column. Eventually, other diocesan newspapers followed suit. And new goals are developing.

Early in my writing ministry, the advice found in Psalm 33 helped me to persevere when the end results of my efforts were uncertain. Transitions, whether wanted or unwanted, exciting or tiresome, happy or sad, are all about singing a new song to the Lord.

When you find yourself facing changes, don't be afraid. Be thankful. Don't give up, give praise. Sing a new song to the Lord. Trust me, before long, a melodious composure will result.

Homeward Bound

"But when they returned to their own land, they didn't go through Jerusalem to report to Herod, for God had warned them in a dream to go home another way." Matthew 2:12

As the New Year starts, I ponder the wise men. Following prophesies, they traveled to Bethlehem to find the Christ child. Afterward, having been warned in a dream to go home another way, they did.

It sounds so simple, doesn't it? But it couldn't have been. Going home another way was illogical. There were no beaten paths, Map-quest, or global positioning systems. They could have gotten lost, encountered risks, or wasted valuable time. Certainly, they didn't know why they felt the urge to choose a new route, but somehow, they knew they had to. Somehow, they believed.

The first time the Lord re-directed me, I doubted.

Our three daughters and I were driving home from dental appointments. The kids, laughing, were exchanging puzzles, bells and whistles, which they had chosen from the dentist's toy basket.

The downtown drive twisted through seedy neighborhoods, past sleazy houses with sagging porches, weedy yards and clotheslines drooping with faded garments.

As I slowed for a red light, I noticed a solitary girl in yellow shorts sitting on the sidewalk. She looked dejected. Her knees were drawn under her chin, her dark arms wrapped around her legs, and her head was buried in the folds of her arms.

Age-wise, the pre-teen could have blended with our family. But the disparity between the giggling kids in my van and the dejected girl at the side of the road struck me.

Most likely, she didn't enjoy excellent health care, financial security or emotional stability. My chattering daughters were rich in family and abundant in blessings, but I bet this girl couldn't depend on a hot meal every night or expect special celebrations in restaurants. The disparity pierced me like a dagger.

I stopped, right beside her, for the traffic light.

Something told me to connect with her, but I didn't know what to do. I suspected she needed an encouraging word, but I didn't know what to say. Something nagged me to share our abundance, but I didn't know what to give.

The traffic signal changed. Despite the urge to help her, I didn't change my route. I went home the way I planned. I swung onto the interstate's eastbound ramp

My Emmaus Walk

and watched the girl in the yellow shorts disappear in my rearview mirror.

Only then did the action of the wise men resonate with me, and I knew I'd made a poor choice.

Divine messages aren't just history. God still speaks to us. Sometimes we're urged to choose a different route. Sometimes we're prompted to go out of our way. How do we respond? We may fear getting lost, encountering risks, or wasting valuable time, but if we can believe and follow, we'll join the ranks of the wise men.

We'll go home a different way and be forever changed.

The Power of a Praying Mother

"Here," my mother-in-law said. "We'll put the documents in these manila folders. The next time you come over, we will finish sorting them."

I was sitting on the floor surrounded by piles of bills, insurance policies, and bank statements. I slipped each stack into a folder, placed the folders in her file case and stood up.

"Where do you want this?" I asked.

She took the case. "Right here," she said.

Mom opened a closet door. The closet was jammed with boxes of every size. At least for now, we shoved the little gray file case inside and pushed the door shut.

Mom sat in her recliner.

I turned toward the sink for a glass of water.

"Would you like a drink?" I asked.

"Sure," she said. "Water, please."

As I reached for a glass, I looked around.

There was a large framed picture of the prayer of St. Francis of Assisi, which hung in her living room. She'd had it for years and every time she moved, it moved with her. *Lord, make me an instrument of your peace.*

The ice clinked into her glass and I filled her cup. Stepping toward her, I handed the drink to her.

She looked back at me with that characteristic twinkle in her eyes and irrepressible hint of a smile on her face.

Where there is hatred, let me sow love. That definitely was my mother-in-law. She lived that prayer.

I thought of all the changes Mom had endured in the past year. Moving here from another town… Losing her beloved husband… Losing her involvement in the church choir…

Yet, she never complained.

I turned around to get a glass of water for myself.

Near the sink I noticed a well-worn plaque. On it was the familiar verse, Psalm 23.

The Lord is my shepherd, I shall not want.

Mom saw me reading it.

"I pray that a lot," she said, smiling.

"The Lord is my shepherd," she began, quietly.

"I shall not want. He makes me lie down in green pastures.

He leads me beside still waters.

He restores my soul."

The familiar words rolled from her lips. She had it memorized.

"He leads me in right paths for his names sake.

Even though I walk through the darkest valley,

I fear no evil.

For you are with me;

Your rod and your staff, they comfort me.
You prepare a table before me
in the presence of my enemies;
You anoint my head with oil,
my cup overflows."

She got up and headed toward the sink, cup in hand.

I turned and faced her. In one unforgettable moment, our eyes met.

"Surely goodness and mercy shall follow me," I watched her say.

I joined her in praying the final lines of the verse.

"all the days of my life,

And I shall live in the house of the Lord forevermore."

CPSIA information can be obtained
at www.ICGtesting.com
Printed in the USA
BVHW08s1122180918
527821BV00001B/128/P